The Top

10

Things

Your Real Estate Agent or Property Manager Won't Tell You

Ethan Walker

Table of Contents

CHAPTER ONE

Top 10 Things the Real Estate Professionals Won't Tell You

Owning assets that generate passive income is a better budgetary methodology than owning resources that generate expenses. In the event that you possess a house or condo for your own living arrangement, for instance, you have to pay for upkeep, repairs, taxes, mortgage, finishing, utilities, or a mortgage holder affiliation expense that covers a portion of these costs. Assuming, nonetheless, you possess a house or flat accessible for leasing or rent, you can generate cash with the property, and now and again, wind up with positive income after all of those costs are paid for. Being a proprietor is a reasonable business; all things considered, landowners exist for each rental occupant, and they frequently flourish fiscally.

Prevailing in the matter of investment properties requires a specific arrangement of abilities and desires, and bringing home the bacon isn't generally as simple as some would think. Should you want to earn a living off of real estate, for instance, what might be called a $50,000 salary equivalent, you'll have to earn more than $4,000 every month. That is a considerable amount of money. Consider these questions and tips before you choose to get into the investment property business to decide whether you have what it takes to be a proprietor.

Do you like "doing it yourself"? Do you know the right people?

Can you handle the 24-hour responsibilities?

Do you like dealing with people?

Do you have the money and reserve funds to purchase the properties?

Can you cover your costs by charging sufficiently high rent?

The lives of real estate professionals are often conflicted. From one viewpoint, they are business people and only profit when their transaction closes. Then again, they are advisors counseling buyers and sellers in real estate business deals. In a perfect world, they should give their customers wholesome guidance irrespective of their own particular budgetary desires.

Frequently, these two goals are in agreement and there is no issue. For instance, the listing agent profits on the chance that he can offer a house for a higher sum. In any case, there are numerous circumstances where the correct guidance for a customer isn't aligned with the

Realtor's financial motivation. For instance, a purchaser's agent profits when his purchasers buy a house for a higher sum.

Regardless of whether you're searching for a venture opportunity or simply a place to live, there are some vital things about purchasing and offering a home that most real estate professionals won't let you know. The top 10 of these are detailed below:

1.You don't have to contact a Realtor to sell your home.

In the event you're willing to look into valuing and can take incredible pictures, you can succeed in selling your home yourself. When the real estate market is booming, you may not need to do much besides buy a "for sale" sign and deal with the offers that come flooding in.

For most FSBO postings, you'll have to get your home onto the Multiple Listing Service (MLS), which is the huge database real estate purchasers and Realtors use to discover homes available to be purchased. Level charge administrations—for example, FSBO or US Realty—enable you to get your home recorded on the MLS without a Realtor; however, you'll have to offer a commission for the purchaser's Realtor.

In case you're offering a house yourself, be aware of its market worth. Underpricing it implies leaving cash on the table; however, a home evaluated too high may never receive an offer.

2.Don't move.

From an absolutely money-related point of view, throughout your life you should move as few times as possible. Let's be honest, moving is costly. When you include the transaction expenses, expenses of moving, expenses to furnish your new residence, and so forth, it's a ton of cash. In addition, in the early stages of satisfying an amortized mortgage contract, your regularly scheduled installment goes, for the most part, to interest. As you hold the home loan longer, your installments progressively go toward paying principal. Deciding not to move is a good way to help you save funds.

3.Your house is not an investment.

How about we allay this legend now: A house is a place to live, not an investment. Beyond a shadow of a doubt, good home proprietorship rates bolster the general economy, driving home value loaning and, subsequently, spending by the normal customer. However, the thought that home possession delivers long-haul venture gains is generally a false notion. What you're basically purchasing is real estate, on the grounds that the structure is a devaluing resource that through the span of a couple of decades could require a huge amount of money in repairs and maintenance. So regardless of whether you purchased your home today for $250,000 and offer it quite a while from now for $500,000, the gain won't be so critical as you may think because of upkeep expenses and inflation.

We buy into the Robert Kiyosaki (author of "Rich Father, Poor Father") mindset and advise our purchasers not to consider their home an investment vehicle. An investment ought to create income. A home does the reverse: it sucks up money. Also, the bigger the home, the more costs it will create: more taxes, more upkeep, and more cash to furniture it, clean it, and so on.

4. More house means more problems.

As a purchaser, you should attempt to locate the simplest home that will make you (and your family) happy. The bigger the home you possess, the more costs you will have. Regardless of whether you are hoping to purchase a two-room, salt-box house or a 6,000-square-foot, five-room home, one key inquiry you ought to consider is whether the house is too huge for your present and future needs.

5. Deal contracts don't offer ironclad assurances.

Each house, except if it's new, has material imperfections. (Some of the time even spic-and-span ones do as well!) And keep in mind that such deformities are ordinarily uncovered and reflected in the deal value. The standard dialect incorporated into most real estate contracts gives purchasers, to an extreme degree, an excess of elbowroom to utilize the intercession procedure to pry more cash out of vendors well after arrangements have been finished. For the record, purchasers need to do their research and analysis so they don't get shortchanged. Be that as it may, sooner or later, the provision of caveat emptor needs to rule. In the event that you are selling a home, have a real estate advisor add an addendum to the contract that will ensure you against future attempts to take cash out of your pockets. Otherwise, it could transform into an endless fight in court and become a financial sinkhole, and in those cases, only the legal advisors win.

6. Home reviewers are not constantly biased.

Most home reviews neglect to mirror the real expense of required repairs. The reason is straightforward: most Realtors don't need those costs known. An exhaustive audit of a devaluing resource such as a home will definitely uncover imperfections – which, obviously, could slaughter or defer a deal. That is the reason Realtors utilize home reviewers who are boosted not to make their employment additionally difficult. Along these lines, purchasers should enlist their own particular home auditor as well as a contractor to gauge everything that shows up in the examination report. Regularly, land operators will offer purchasers an apparently liberal single amount to cover any required upkeep, yet it's never enough.

7. Commissions are debatable.

In this age, where some alluring listings get various money offers quickly, it borders on craziness for a dealer to pay a Realtor a commission of 5–6 percent. The average deals cost for a home in Los Angeles is moving toward $700,000, as indicated by Trulia. That implies a Realtor's take could be as high as $40,000. While I'm not endeavoring to make anybody bankrupt, there is by all accounts a crucial discrepancy between that level of pay and the measure of work required to bring a deal to a close – particularly given that online gateways—for example, Zillow—are making this procedure substantially less demanding than at any other time in history. The issue is that the Multiple Listing Service (MLS) framework, which apparently is planned to make property exchanges more effective for all parties, is basically an imposing business model.

8. You may not like your neighbors.

Everybody realizes that the most imperative thing about a property is location, location, location. Be that as it may, shouldn't something be said about the neighbors? I've experienced the home-purchasing process a couple of times, and never has a land specialist said to me, "Hello, investigate and meet your potential neighbors." Why? Since they knew I might not have liked what I found. Neighbors are a particularly essential thought in the event that you are considering purchasing an apartment suite. Those dividers can be paper thin. It would be unfortunate to put cash into a place just to have an animosity-fraught relationship with somebody who is just feet away. Invest some energy and get a sense of who would be living nearby.

9.You need not pay a commission in the event that you bring your own purchaser.

So you're signing your agreement with a Realtor tomorrow, and your neighbor's friend or cousin's manager has effectively assessed the place. When you sign the agreement, if the manager makes an offer, you'll need to contact your Realtor. Isn't that so?

One moment. Before you sign with the Realtor, disclose in writing any authentic potential purchasers who've effectively shown interest. In the event that a disclosed purchaser chooses to finish the buy, you don't need to go through the Realtor ... or pay the agent's bonus.

10.That warranty is useless

Property developers and the Realtors who speak for them may offer warranties on new home development. Ansbacher, the Florida lawyer, says purchasers are absurd to place much solace in such assurances. Be careful when reviewing the standard contract for any new build you are thinking about becoming tied up with.

All developer contracts incorporate a waiver of the right to sue, which implies you-know-who will bear the expense of repairs for poor development. Get your own legal advisor to pinpoint that bothersome condition and arrange it out of the agreement.

Aside from the above things, when buying land properties, there are a few things that individuals don't consider with regards to costs. Costs that are incurred while creating rental income and amid the time of occupancy may be claimed as a tax deduction. A portion of these costs is admissible while others are non-permissible rental costs (you are required to keep the supporting documents for about five years for confirmation purposes).

The sorts of costs are housing loans, property insurance, property tax, repairs, cost of securing an occupant, upkeep, furniture and fittings, cost of supervision and administration expenses, web charges/costs, costs acquired on properties that are not generating rental income, and utility costs.

Housing loan is the interest paid on the mortgage or home loan taken out to buy the property that is leased; property tax comes about during the rental time frame; fire insurance is the premiums paid for protection against fire incidents.

CHAPTER TWO

Become Your Own Real Estate Agent

If you have at some point planted a "for sale" sign in your front yard, you've at least thought about selling your home without a real estate broker. Why would it be a good idea to offer someone whose services are only a little better than Multiple Listing Services 5 or 6 percent of the price of your house sale? (On a $400,000 house, that's $24,000.)

Choosing to become a Realtor is a noteworthy move in anybody's career. Individuals enter the field of real estate from different occupations and professions, and at different phases of their lives. Everybody has distinctive reasons why they think real estate is the right vocation decision for them. Be that as it may, one question continuously asked by individuals hoping to enter the real estate business is: "How would I become my own real estate agent?"

It's an inquiry that's all the more important given the depreciating real estate market. With the measure of value in numerous homes on the decrease, the potential investment funds make a truly solid case for the for-sale-by-owner (FSBO) approach.

In reality, by leaving Realtors out of the equation, homeowners could slice their asking price by about 3–4 percent below similar listings in their neighborhood, helping them offer their home quicker, and still win out over the competition.

The basic answer to the question of how to become your own Realtor is, it depends. For the most part, it relies upon where an individual wants to own real estate. A state license is required to become a real estate agent. Each state controls their own property licensing process, and each state's rules or regulations are somewhat different. Be that as it may, there are a couple of essential prerequisites that are constant.

General Requirements to Qualify to Become a Real Estate Salesperson

To qualify to end up as an authorized land salesman or operator, you should:

1. Be no less than 18 or 19 years of age (varies from state to state)

2. Have lawful U.S. residency

3. Complete your state pre-license education

4. Pass your state land permit examination

While these things are necessary for your journey towards becoming a real estate agent, there are a lot of choices you have to make along the way that will determine whether you will be ahead of the game.

Are You Fit for the Real Estate Market?

The initial phase in this procedure is ensuring that the real estate business is appropriate for you. As a Realtor, every day is spent working for you. This implies taking care of your own office administration, doing your own paperwork, chasing leads, building a network, overseeing contracts, and managing purchasers and dealers. Contact your neighborhood Realtors and get some information about what the everyday work looks like. Make inquiries about real estate as a long-term profession. Beginning a full-time vocation as a Realtor can't be dealt with like a pastime. It requires full responsibility and commitment.

Becoming a Real Estate Agent

While the specifics differ by state, there are five stages that each individual must go through to procure their permit and become a real estate agent.

Stage 1: *Understand Your State's Real Estate Licensing Requirements*

Each state's property licensing prerequisites are unique. Your state's real estate commission website will list the formal pre-licensing necessities.

Stage 2: *Enroll in a Real Estate Pre-licensing Course*

There are a number of ways you can choose to complete your property pre-licensing education prerequisites, from live classroom instruction at nearby real estate schools; real estate licensing programs from some realty firms, colleges, and technical schools; home-study; and online real estate training. This is a vital choice in your adventure. Ensure you enlist in a school that has a decent reputation, offers quality substance and educators, and is centered on positive understudy results.

Stage 3: *Apply to Take the Real Estate Agent Exam*

Timing is imperative at this stage. Ensure you are following the application procedure with your state so you can sit for your Realtor exam not long after you complete your real estate licensing classes. This procedure will be particular to your state and comes with a fee. Check with your state's Realtor specialist for all pertinent details. A few states require you to submit fingerprints and pass a personal investigation. This can take a long time to process. In numerous states, the application procedure must be finished before you can register your exam date. Try not to give the paperwork a chance to end up being a barrier to beginning your new career.

Stage 4: Pass the Real Estate Agent Exam

Passing the real estate exam takes more than completing the educational prerequisites—it takes planning. Not every person passes the exam on the first try. Setting yourself up to pass the state exam takes extra study time. Taking practice exams, estimating your strengths and shortcomings, and working through far-reaching topical reviews will hone your insight and set you up for exam day.

Stage 5: *Find a Real Estate Broker*

Your passing evaluation on your state real estate licensing exam doesn't exactly mean you have a permit yet. Consider finding a real estate broker from the get-go in your licensing procedure. When you have finished your pre-licensing educational prerequisites and passed your exam, you and your broker will both need to complete final paperwork with the state. Once the form is acknowledged, your license will be issued, and you may practice real estate under the sponsorship of the broker.

Benefits of Acting as One's Own Real Estate Agent

Taking care of real estate business yourself places you in control. You won't need to stress about if an agent is consulting with your best interests in mind. The transactions are your obligation, regardless of whether they are fruitful or not. In the event that you are an effective communicator and a people-person, you can do this.

Swift decision-making

The procedure can, in some cases, be taken care of all the more rapidly without an agent. You may locate the ideal house or bit of property to purchase; however, your agent is away for the end of the week, which implies somebody may grab it up before you can put in an offer. Being your own real estate agent gives you a chance to send in an offer within a short time of seeing it. This could be essential in booming markets, for example, in San Francisco or San Jose. As an offering agent, you can react rapidly to offers, instead of waiting to have your agent pass on your reaction.

More money is saved

Numerous individuals act as their own real estate agents on account of the commission funds. In all property deals, agents get a commission for their work. Average commissions go from 4–6 percent and are shared between the purchasing and offering agents. This implies that, in the event you go about as your own buying agent, you can lessen your offer by half of the commission sum on the grounds that the seller won't need to pay commission to a purchaser's agent. Likewise, going about as your own offering specialist enables you to diminish your asking cost by 3–4 percent; this could help attract more potential purchasers.

CHAPTER THREE

Things to Look Out For When Buying a Rental Property

Hoping to expand your investment and exploit the present real estate market prices? While in no way a laid-back asset, investing in real estate offers a few favorable circumstances. Commercial real estate property investments can give extra short- and long-term income and noteworthy tax breaks also.

However, the trap is in the purchasing. Making a mistake at this basic stage is one you'll pay for over and over during the life of the property. It's critical to be a very educated and mindful purchaser, setting aside the time to do the essential research. There are certain things you should take note of when buying a rental property as they could make or break the deal. A number of these things are discussed in the following section.

1. Go for simple constructions

That Victorian home you've been gazing at may include exquisite leaded glass windows; however, you'll never locate a reasonable substitution at the neighborhood home reno store. A slate rooftop is a delightful thing to see, but it can be frightfully costly to repair. What's more, if the rooftop is extremely steep, expenses could go up considerably further.

Search for a house that has simple, basic construction and uses generally standard materials, where everything is anything but difficult to get to. These are by and large the least demanding and most economical to keep up.

2.Bigger isn't in every case better

As your property size and area help to decide your tax rate, a greater amount of land truly isn't vital. Beyond expanding by and large property estimation, it won't do much as far as rental income goes, except if you have plans to construct an expansion or another rentable structure on the side.

Additionally, the room size won't in any reasonable way affect the rental income. In as much as you meet the minimum requirements of the city or township, an increase in each room's size is not needed. Three small- to medium-sized rooms may generate more rental income than two huge rooms.

3. Utilities can become burdensome

Utilities can be a noteworthy issue for landowners if not set up appropriately. In the event that you supply utilities to your occupants, you, for the most part, can't put them out for defaulting or other issues. In the event that you do, the punishments can be extreme.

Would you want to keep the bills in your name while you have the occupants pay their bit to you? If so, be aware that the law does not, for the most part, enable you to collect in the event that they default on these payments, so you may be at a disadvantage if the occupants stop paying their part of the utility. Besides, you are as yet required to provide them with these utilities, regardless of whether they pay or not.

Except in cases when you can include a fixed charge into the monthly rent figure, which covers your costs even as costs keep on rising, it is best to demand that occupants pay for utilities specifically, under their own names. That way, you are not liable in any case of a default.

4. Make a purchase at the right price

A good deal today will assist you with variances in property estimation after some time. That way, you can benefit if (and when) you decide to sell. You have to build up a profound comprehension of what establishes a property as being of value in the neighborhood(s) in which you're looking. As an investor, you can continue making lowball offers and sit tight for the deals you desire. Investors, nonetheless, generally rush at incredible deals. Thus, you should have the capacity to act rapidly when a property meets your standards.

You likewise need to benchmark rental costs for similar units in the territory. The neighborhood classifieds are an awesome starting point for this. A couple of long periods of research should give you a decent understanding of what you can charge. Simply make a point to factor in for utilities (electric, gas, oil, water, sewer, link, and so on.), in the event that they'll be incorporated into the lease.

5. The right neighborhood to invest

By and large, it's imperative to find a neighborhood where your investment property will have a decent possibility of being rented out. The ritziest corner of town may not be it. Then again, it's difficult to keep great occupants in bad neighborhoods, where crime rates might be higher. Your presence in the area should improve it as a place.

Notwithstanding which neighborhood you pick, you never need your property to be the most noticeably bad-looking one. Not only will this affect your rentability, but objections and potentially citations may arrive as well.

If you have picked a property which noticeably needs repairs, you should spend money and time to address these issues in the principal year, and preferably before leasing it. This demonstrates to the township or city authorities that you're one of the great landowners, focused on keeping your property up. It can have a gigantic effect on your encounters over the life of the property. Every property you claim reflects your work, capacities, and responsibility.

6.Know about neighborhood rental laws and regulations

In numerous areas, rental properties are dealt with more like organizations than living arrangements. This can prompt many (costly) shocks, in the event that you don't do your research in advance.

For instance: while eight-by-ten may pass for a legitimate room in your own home, it likely won't be viewed as such for an investment property.

It is safe to assume that you'll have to upgrade your property into agreement with neighborhood rental regulations before you gain any income from the property. So it would be wise to carry out the necessary research in order to avoid being caught unaware after having paid for a property.

CHAPTER FOUR

The Magic of Section 8

What is Section 8?

The Housing Choice Voucher Program, financed by the U.S. Department of Housing and Urban Development, is laid out in Section 8 of the Housing Act of 1937, and therefore Section 8 has moved toward becoming shorthand for the program.

The concept of Section 8 is moderately basic: rather than cash being spent to fabricate public housing, the money is given to families as vouchers that cover part or the majority of the expense of leasing from a private proprietor. Investment properties that acknowledge members in the Housing Choice Voucher Program are known as Section 8 housing.

The Section 8 program enables private proprietors to lease apartments and homes at decent rates to qualified low-income tenants, giving them a chance to choose for themselves what tradeoffs they need to make around building quality, location, cost, and the various applicable variables.

The Advantages of Renting to Section 8 Tenants

1. Consistent rent payment by the government

Section 8 provides rental help and it's a government-run program. Prospective tenants apply for the program, and in the event that they meet certain prerequisites, the government gives them a housing voucher. This voucher enables them to search for housing within a specific price limit. Once the rental unit has been affirmed and reviewed by the nearby Public Housing

Authority, you can sign a rental agreement with the occupant. The Public Housing Authority is in charge of paying the occupant's housing voucher specifically to the proprietor every month.

Leasing to a Section 8 inhabitant gives the upside of getting the rental installment reliably every month. The Public Housing Authority will either mail you a check or they will send the sum straight into your account.

At times an occupant is still in charge of paying a small part of the lease and should pay this segment specifically to you. Section 8 tenants realize that any infringement of the terms of the rent contract, including paying rent, could result in the loss of their Section 8 voucher. In this manner, they have a solid motivating force to pay their portion of the lease every month.

2. Consistent tenant base

Another perk of permitting Section 8 tenants in your property is that you are opening up to a formerly undiscovered occupant base. You are opening your property to a steady occupant base and, in addition, widening your inhabitant base.

Section 8 vouchers are popular all across the country. Numerous territories have a long waiting list of individuals who long to be on the program. Consequently, you don't need to stress that there will be a lack of Section 8 occupants. Regardless of whether your market does not have an extensive number of inhabitants on Section 8, by accepting these occupants, you are not depending on them as the best way to fill your opportunity; rather, you are simply expanding your prospective tenant pool.

3. Targeted marketing

Section 8 affords you the opportunity to make use of marketing opportunities that you might not have initially had access to or used. It provides you with in-person and online marketing opportunities. When showcasing your property to Section 8 tenants, you have the opportunity to post fliers in your neighborhood Public Housing Authority Office alongside other customary advertising alternatives. This comes at no cost. You could also publicize your rental on the Internet, promote your property on conventional sites like Craigslist and Trulia, and on a dedicated site devoted to Section 8 tenants.

4. Pre-screened tenants

The Section 8 tenants have been pre-screened and must have met the prerequisites for Section 8 housing before they are presented with housing vouchers. The Section 8 office concentrates their screening on the occupant's pay level. Notwithstanding, they regularly reveal different issues while performing this wage screening—for example, a criminal history. Public Housing Authorities won't give Housing Choice Vouchers to individuals who have been ousted because of drug-related activities in the last three years.

The Public Housing Authority is required to provide the proprietor with the following data:

1. The kind of screening they have led on the inhabitant.
2. The occupant's present and past addresses.
3. The name and addresses of the inhabitant's present and past proprietors.

Segment 8 conducts this fundamental screening for you, yet you should not depend entirely on their screening. You should perform your own intensive screenings on your

occupants, including Section 8 occupants. This ought to include a credit check and record verification.

5. Increased rents

Once every year, landowners are permitted to reassess lease installments they get from inhabitants, which means they can charge their Section 8 occupants higher rental expenses.

A proprietor is expected to follow the law and in the event that he/she is leasing to Section 8 inhabitants, the proprietor must follow the statewide landlord-tenant law and extra guidelines set on him or her by the Section 8 program. Some responsibilities proprietors are charged with include:

- Ascertaining if you are required to accept Section 8 tenants.
- Selecting a Section 8 tenant that also meets your personal standards.
- Passing your property quality standards inspection.
- Notifying Section 8 of an increase in lease.
- Adherence to the terms of the lease contract.
- Collecting security deposit and monthly rent.

CHAPTER FIVE

Do Not Buy a Super-Expensive Property to Rent Out

With regards to real estate property, the more you spend, the more cash everybody makes. The costs begin to accrue from the very moment you find the "perfect property." Maintaining a rental property can be costly. Property taxes must be paid, and the property must be kept up. Repairs must be done promptly. Sometimes, proprietors may wind up with occupants who ruin the property or neglect to pay the lease, and it very well may be a long procedure to evict them.

One of the basic techniques associated with acquiring and owning rental properties is utilizing leverage. In a perfect situation, you will buy a property basically utilizing borrowed cash. And immediately, the income from the property won't just pay the home loan, but likewise, furnish you with a little profit. Over numerous years, that income will develop, and your home loan will get smaller. In the long run, you will have a property that is a virtual money machine. Leverage is a key instrument for each and every real estate investor. However, there are times when a proprietor should pay off the mortgage on time.

A great many people get a 30-year home loan and pay that regularly scheduled installment until the point when the cows come home. Sadly, that often implies they never truly make much rental income until they are old.

Luckily, it doesn't need to be that way. Clearly, the lower the mortgage you incur, the quicker you might have the capacity to pay it off. Also, when you purchase a house that is on the lower end of your budget plan, you may even have the capacity to bear the cost of the regularly scheduled installment on an advance with a shorter term.

Your mortgage doesn't have to be forever. Envision paying off your mortgage in 15 years and the freedom and rental income that would afford you. Huge, costly houses may have their own advantages; however, being without debt or with as low an amount of debt as possible will be extremely valuable.

Know Your Risk Tolerance

You have to come to terms with the risk you're willing to put up with and what your limits are. Your financial risk tolerance (the level of financial vulnerability you will condone to accomplish possibly more prominent rewards) is dictated by a blend of components, including your investment objectives and experience, how much time you need to contribute, your other money-related assets and your "fear factor."

You can determine your financial risk tolerance by asking yourself the following questions:

- Are you more worried about losing cash or missing out on an adventurous opportunity?
- How much cash are you comfortable losing?
- How stressed do you figure you would be in a serious market price slump?
- What sorts of investment might keep you up at night?

Avoid Mortgages as Much as Possible

While avoiding as much debt as possible is the rule of thumb every rental property owner should subscribe to, there are times when an early payment of a property's mortgage is the most logical thing to do. Some of those cases include:

When cash flow is in the red

If the mortgage payment each month is more than the rental income, implying negative cash flow and invariably financing your occupant's residency. This situation can be turned around by clearing the mortgage.

When you require income rather than the tax benefit

Ordinarily, the explanation behind owning investment property is to produce tax benefits. Those benefits diminish your tax obligation on other income sources.

In the event that you require an actual income property, you stand a better chance of achieving this if you pay off the mortgage.

When you need to resign

It is generally good practice to pay off all debts once you reach retirement. With this in mind, settling the home loan on your rental property might be a surprisingly better long- term wager. This is particularly valid if it is believed that the stock market is heading down, or is entering what could turn out to be a long-term bear market trend. Satisfying a 6 percent contract on a rental property could turn out to be preferable when contrasted with a market in which you may lose at least 25 percent of your stock portfolio in the following three or four years.

CHAPTER SIX

Real Estate Property Management

Buying into properties can be productive, yet it involves a considerable measure of work. Successful investors must manage everything from dealing with their cash to dealing with their properties—something that, much of the time, appears significantly less demanding than it really is. This is the reason the best investors quite often work with real estate property managers. Proper property management is an essential piece of all worthwhile investments, and something that property investors ought to have.

Property management is defined by the business dictionary as the process of managing property that is available for lease by maintaining and handling all day-to-day activities that are centered on the piece of real estate.

The property manager or management company has four noteworthy regions of obligation:

- Tenant and occupancy
- Finances and marketing
- Facility management
- Administration and risk management

The real estate property manager is the proprietor's associate and helps in making the most return on investment through the productive execution of these four utilitarian territories of obligation. The property manager acts in the best interests of the proprietor to keep up the property, fill it with occupants, gather rents, spend on improvements, and keep records. It's unquestionably a specialty for the more meticulous and responsive in the profession.

Tenancy and Occupancy

Grasping the needs of the occupants is imperative for a successful property manager. Motivating them to move in is just the start. The real estate manager should then react to their solicitations, oversee their activities with respects to the rent necessities, collect the loan in time, and ceaselessly survey the occupants' satisfaction with respect to the property's facilities compared to those of competitors in the same location. The unwelcome undertaking of removal for infringement or non-payment is a piece of this capacity as well.

Finances and Marketing

Property management includes a comprehension of working costs and planning. From this data, proper rental rates are set, adjusted by the present market and what it will support in the way of rents. Very detailed information regarding the territory and rival rental properties is needed.

The property supervisor may endorse advertising programs, special promotions, and other promotional techniques to the proprietor with a specific end goal to expand occupancy and rental rates. Consistent financial review with the proprietors is required. Understanding fiscal statements, profit and loss, tax assessment, and budget planning are essential for the property manager.

Facility Management

Property management also incorporates the physical management of the structures and the outdoor facilities. Finishing, electrical, plumbing, rooftop, walls, machines, and substantially more are all part of the physical property. The property director must keep up associations with independent contractors and repair organizations, plan for expenses, and assess the condition of maintenance and repair works.

This capacity works hand in hand with the financial arm, as a few upgrades will require substantial capital expenses and planning for them. It's in accord with the tenancy and occupancy management since it is vital for occupant retention to have properties that are very much looked after.

Administration and Risk Management

This is the documentation and recording aspect of the real estate management work. Federal, state, and local governments all have some control over property management activities. Certain necessities must be met for every one of them. Careful records of bookkeeping and taxes are an absolute necessity.

For reasons of risk, all interactions and occupant dealings must be recorded and kept up for indicated periods. In spite of the fact that this is related to financial functions, there are exceptionally inflexible prerequisites in many states for the treatment of assets paid by leaseholders for payment to proprietors.

In New Mexico, property management accounted by a long shot for the most buyer dissensions and disciplinary activities by the real estate commission. Dissimilar to most property transactions when you are speaking for a side of the transaction, property management includes managing property proprietors and occupants. Property management in New Mexico represented the most license suspensions, too. The multifaceted nature and elements of managing proprietors and inhabitants add to the risk.

What Qualities Should a Property Manager Possess?

Having arrived at a conclusion of what the responsibility of a real estate property manager should be, it would be apt to consider the particular character traits and qualities that would aid in carrying out these responsibilities.

A property supervisor must be a skilled performer of numerous undertakings, keeping the proprietors and occupants happy. Notwithstanding keeping a property in good shape and appealing, a property supervisor is in charge of safeguarding the value of the property. Albeit just a secondary school confirmation is required for this position, many customers want to contact a property manager with a degree in business, finance or real estate. An abundance of other professional qualities is essential for a property manager to be successful The most important ones to look out for when employing or selecting a real estate property manager are:

1. Education and experience
2. People skills and solid relational abilities
3. Detail-orientation
4. Organizational qualities
5. An investor's outlook
6. Patience
7. Aggressiveness
8. Flexibility
9. Ingenuity
10. Technology awareness

CHAPTER SEVEN

PropertyRader and All the Neat Little Gadgets That Real Estate Agents Have

A lot of things have changed in the real estate industry over the course of recent years. On account of cutting-edge technology, we are now able to establish further the process of offering and purchasing a home. Besides, experts can utilize a wide range of applications and devices to keep their teams and tasks organized. Regardless of whether you're in search of a property on sale or hoping to get a lease in the area, now you can do it without putting any distance between you and your customers. Smart gadgets facilitate the process of managing the property, and they should be incorporated into a real estate broker's everyday portfolio.

Improving the process of investing in real estate doesn't need to be that stressful. Innovation has progressed massively, and we can now utilize it to make things run smoother by a considerable measure. iPads and tablets enable real estate agents to remain connected round the clock. Cell phones also help in this regard, and presently, we utilize the cloud to keep funds, get live updates and reports, and to wrap things up. A few organizations even utilize drones to photograph districts and furnish potential purchasers with a present-state view of accessible properties. We've overcome so much that we can't stop.

PropertyRadar is one such tool that has come to make the process of real estate prospecting very stress-free and fun. PropertyRadar helps you find, know, and connect with every best potential customer in your market; it makes targeted local marketing effective and affordable. Presently, it prides itself on being the most comprehensive local prospecting, data, knowledge, and marketing app that has ever been made for small businesses.

Its service is presently available in California, Arizona, Nevada, Oregon, and Washington, and it costs on average $39 per month to subscribe to this service. PropertyRadar helps you to:

- Find new customers and conduct market research easily.
- Know it all by providing you with the detailed customer and prospect research.
- Connect across channels.
- Automate sales and marketing.

PropertyRadar is used by a large number of small local businesses, some of which are real estate investors, real estate agents, real estate professionals, home services and so on.

Aside from PropertyRadar, there are some other exceptional gadgets that can revolutionize the real estate business and would be very helpful to real estate agents. The most prominent of these gadgets include:

Revolutionary Desk

Many real estate agents spend a lot of time behind a desk. They're accountable for performing many various tasks, utilizing loads of devices. To help make things less demanding for them, it would be a smart thought to put resources into a cutting-edge work area. EXODesk is a spic-and-span item that will reform the manner in which individuals work together while sitting at a work area. The monster "mammoth table screen work area" invites clients to connect their iOS gadgets to the work area; at that point, they can see and perform activities utilizing the work area as a virtual console and independent gadget. The EXODesk can be changed over into a giant schedule, enabling users to be more organized.

Amazon Echo

Amazon Echo has already made a name for itself in the global real estate industry. The most famous gadget in the Voice-Activated Internet (VAI) space is being talked about for its viability as a lead generator. In any case, there is no contending that having your brand or company suggested by Alexa makes for a smooth piece of showcasing panache. Voiceter Pro and Agent Neo are at the top of the ladder in this space.

Ghost 2 Quadrocopter

To a great degree simple to utilize and exceptionally smart, the Phantom 2 quadrocopter is a gadget each real estate agent should possess. It tends to be utilized to photograph properties from a distance of up to 300 meters. The gadget is connected to Wi-Fi and with its stable drifting property you can stop it in the air to take photographs, or zoom in to get certain property particularities. The gadget likewise has a video stream capacity, and it is fantastic at evaluating areas, as well. Completely charged, the Phantom 2 can last up to 25 minutes of flight time. The cost is evaluated at $150.

Gnarbox Portable Backup Drive and Editor

This is the for the new-gen Realtors who utilize drones and 3D tours to advertise postings. This gadget simplifies a lot of things. The burly, postcard-sized Gnarbox quickly synchronizes and composes photographs and video content from any camera or gadget. It comes with installed Wi-Fi to stream data and has 128 GB or 256 GB of storage capacity.

Apple AirPods

In case your vehicle still isn't interfacing your calls, it's an ideal opportunity to get your hands on the Apple AirPods. They are compact and charge while stowed in their dental floss-sized case. They are the best choice for your mobile listing center. By merely opening the case, a pairing process is triggered.

In the event that it is Apple-on-Apple, Siri is available in two speedy taps. It is exceptionally valuable when trying to locate a potential posting or affirm an arrangement time while in a hurry.

Pocket Printer

Real estate professionals handle a considerable measure of printed material daily. They regularly require duplicates of various reports, but since they're in a hurry, they don't generally have access to a printer or scanner. The Pocket Printer can be an exceptionally helpful gadget. It was first released on Kickstarter and it turned out to be progressive. Essentially, the gadget scans records; then, it stores them so you can print them straight from a laptop, cell phone, or tablet.

Powermat

It's a well-known fact that cell phones use up a great deal of battery power. Realtors, specifically, put in a lot of time chatting on the telephone. They can't stand to come up short on battery. Likewise, they don't generally have time to recharge their cell phones, especially when in a hurry. Luckily, Powermat was conceived. The cordless charging framework from Duracell is amazing. It is compatible with many gadgets, and to charge your telephone you simply put the phone on the mat. It's as basic as that. Powermat plans to wind up the Wi-Fi of power, helping business in various fields keep their gadgets completely charged throughout the day.

CHAPTER EIGHT

New Tenants

There are great tenants and there are terrible tenants.

While no screening strategy is flawless, there are some factors you should consider which will increase your chances of finding an ideal occupant for your rental property. In the event you attend to all of this counsel, you are substantially more liable to get a decent occupant, which makes your job as a proprietor much less demanding. Try not to do this midway. The value you'll pay over the rent term due to a poor occupant decision is simply too high.

Meet with them in person

You will need to physically meet them and walk them through the property. Seeing your imminent tenant in person can give you some critical information. You'll get a feeling of their cleanliness by observing what they drive, and the premonition you get about them is extremely valuable. It requires next to no investment to set up a property showcase, so ensure you don't miss this.

Trust your instincts

You can do all the screening on the planet; however, now and again, your senses are the best judge of character. You may feel that there is something off about an occupant who generally looks great on paper. Trust your screening, yet don't overlook your gut.

Check their references.

This means calling their last two landlords, their boss, and their own references. Try not to slack on this. You'll need to have real discussions with these individuals. This aids in painting a superior picture of what your tenant-to-be is like.

Inquiries you should make include:

- Did the tenant pay their lease on time?
- What was the explanation behind the move?
- Was the occupant removed for non-payment of the lease or for defying the proprietor's guidelines?
- Did the inhabitant give 30 days' notice before moving?
- How did they keep their apartment? Is it safe to say that they were clean?
- Did they cause any harm to the property other than ordinary wear and tear?
- Were they in harmony with and respectful of their neighbors?
- Did they complain frequently?

Pick a Tenant Who Is Stable

Take a closer look at the tenant's earlier addresses and work history on their application form. Do they move or switch occupations regularly? In the event that they move frequently, this is probably going to happen again and you will before long have a vacant rental property staring you in the face once more. If they have not had stable employment over time, they will most likely be unable to bear the cost of the rental property in three months and you will be left managing an ousting or beginning your tenant search all over again.

Take a large deposit

You'll need to take a significant deposit that will really cover harms in the event that your occupant ends up being a bad apple. One key tip is to never make the deposit the same as their month-to-month rent payment. For example, if the lease is $2,000 you ought to request $2,500 as a deposit. In the event that you request a deposit similar to the lease sum, your inhabitant will probably expect that it covers their last month's lease. You don't need that.

Follow the law

Proprietors must treat every single prospective occupant similarly. There is a law, known as the Federal Fair Housing Act, which is intended to forestall oppressing certain classes of individuals in any action identified with housing. To put it plainly, you shouldn't discriminate based on:

- Sex
- Nationality
- Religion
- Race
- Familial status (families with youngsters)
- Disability

Moreover, numerous states have their own Fair Housing Rules that you should heed, so ensure you know and live up to your neighborhood laws also.

Pick a tenant with good credit

You need to search for an occupant who is fiscally dependable. In the event that they are dependable with paying their bills, there is a good chance they will pay their lease on time and be responsible for your property. This is a two-step process:

- Verify the tenant's income
- Run a credit check

Do a criminal background check of the prospective tenants

Criminal data is an open record and can be seen at different courthouses. This check will turn up both genuine and minor offenses. You will require the tenant's name and date of birth to run one. Remember that those with a criminal record may endeavor to distort this data, so make a point to check a legitimate ID to confirm that they are who they say they are.

A thorough criminal check will include:

- Federal court record search
- A statewide criminal record search
- A county criminal court search
- A Department of Corrections offender search
- Sexual offender database search

Certain states, for example, California, restrict property owners from refusing tenants with certain criminal past dealings. As a landlord, you may have a simpler time advocating your dismissal of a forthcoming occupant with a drug or vicious crime conviction than you would dismiss an inhabitant with fifty speeding tickets. This is on the grounds that drugs or violent crimes can endanger the wellbeing of other occupants. Also, there is no general database of criminal records, so it might be difficult to complete an exhaustive personal investigation.

Since doing a criminal record check yourself can be extremely tedious, it might be best to employ a legitimate occupant screening organization to carry out this check for you. It can frequently be joined with the credit check, for an extra charge.

CHAPTER NINE

Just Start With One

Investing in real estate is a good way to begin your property portfolio and get in on receiving rental income. Purchasing your first investment property is a noteworthy venture and can be a lucrative one. However, take it from the experts that a few safeguards ought to be taken. Do your research and take as much time as is needed. Being impatient on a property deal can be an expensive lesson for purchasers to learn. You could wind up with a venture that costs significantly more than you expected.

Times of stress and demand—for instance, the beginning of each new year and the end of each monetary year—can take a toll, both mentally and physically, on even the most experienced of property proprietors and novices should be additionally cautious to prevent being burnt out when purchasing the property.

While there's no lack of data accessible about what maturing investors ought to do so as to guarantee success, more critical are the traps to avoid so you don't become one of the people who partake in the real estate industry but aren't successful.

Budding real estate investors are advised to avoid the temptation of buying more than one real estate property to start; this is to prevent them from becoming inundated with the rigors of managing the property, the attendant cash flow or expenses that accompany rental properties that they might not have been trained to see and as a result might not have made provisions for, to prevent them from burning out, and to ensure that they master the industry while being exposed to as little risk as possible. In addition to starting out with a single property, budding investors should take heed of certain things when they go about searching for that one property to buy:

Try not to be too eager

When searching for your first venture property, it's important not to "chase the deal." I regularly observe first-time property investors who overpay for the property since they are so fired up and want to begin. Always know your numbers, and never surpass the correct cost price amid the fervor of bartering or while consulting with home merchants.

Do the math

Give the numbers a chance to speak for themselves. New rental proprietors frequently begin overanalyzing and overcomplicating things. It is pointless. Simply figure it out. In the event that you lease the property out for "X" every month, will you, in any event, earn back the original investment? If you will, at that point the house is a decent arrangement. If not, look elsewhere.

Spend time at the property

Before you commit to your first rental property deal, sit in your car outside the property from 6 a.m. to 9 a.m., and also 9 p.m. You will perceive and better understand what is truly happening in the community you're about to make an investment in.

Work with a finance professional

Your first investment in the property shouldn't be handled solely by you. Keep in touch with experts that comprehend leverage and opportunity cost in the financing scene. Genuine experts will have the capacity to help you in understanding the financing side and what the money-saving advantages are. They will likewise have the capacity to furnish you with information on what the real revolving expense for the property would be and what your actual margins are.

Check the property's value

Whenever you buy a property in the County Appraisal District, odds are you made a good deal. Obviously different variables become integral factors: repairs, upgrades, and so forth. Be that as it may, follow this technique and you will make good returns on your investment.

Buy single-family homes first

Put resources into single-family homes first since it's the least complex approach to begin as a new property investor. The upkeep is less demanding than multi-family or commercial properties. With just one tenant, there typically isn't as much wear and tear on the property, and when something breaks, you'll just need to fix one property.

Make the deal with your head, not your heart

First-time real estate investors don't have the advantage of obtaining a speculation property on a "gut" feeling. Truth be told, you likely need to make the purchase on a greater margin to account for everything you know, the things you don't know, and a buffer well beyond that. Purchasing investment property can be costly, so a couple of terrible decisions could deplete your resources and take you out of the game. You should only purchase a property if the numbers are reasonable.

Consider the location

As a first-time investor in property, the key fundamental of real estate is location, location, location. In the event that you purchase a property that "sustains itself," i.e., covers for government tax, insurance, and upkeep in addition to giving some free income, the odds are, given some more time, that the property appreciation will give great return on investment, consequently providing for chances to renegotiate higher rental wages and deal costs.

CHAPTER TEN

JUST DO IT

Start where you are.
Use what you have.
Do what you can.
— *Arthur Ashe*

Arthur Ashe put it best when he shared these contemplations about going up against challenges. Whether facing an adversary on the tennis court or endeavoring to realize radical change in your life, I speculate that similar standards apply.

Attempting to accomplish something is hard. Combating difficulty as we take a shot at a venture, real estate prospecting, or just in everyday life is considerably harder. Living a better life and making good progress requires seeing past the dissatisfactions and fears that strike on a daily basis. Trusting the process necessitates that we set aside disappointments over outcomes and upgrades that come inconsistently and on a smaller scale than may be desirable.

There will never be an ideal time for you to make a move. There will never be an ideal time for you to go check out that property listing, to spend time with your family, to perform that market analysis, to put a call through to that real estate broker, to make the meeting. When you recognize this, you will get significantly more important work done regularly.

Moving beyond the greatest obstacle

The greatest obstacle for a significant number of us is simply beginning. Deciding to take a step. You can be as successful and effective as you can possibly imagine; all you need to do is take that step of faith and step out of your comfort zone.

You have all that you need to make a change in your niche and in the real estate business industry; you need to get past the excuses you've been telling yourself. All you need to do is find what you are passionate about and go for it.

Try not to think too far into what's to come. Utilize what you have right now at where you are, and witness your creative power come to life.

Find the right property and buy at the right price

Purchasing investment property is a huge financial decision. What you need is a property that will enable you to create enough rental income in the years ahead with minimal stress. The ideal property should have these basic features:

Value appreciation

Most properties have a solid inclination to increase in value over time. The level of property appreciation depends intensely on inflation, location, market, condition, and the neighborhood where the property is located.

Affordability

The cost of purchasing your house should not be so large that it would result in a negative cash flow on the property.

Accessibility

The property should be readily accessible to your target market. Remember, the core tenet of the real estate industry is location, location, location.

Take a chance

Avoid procrastinating on the task. You don't need to have a foolproof plan before you set out to achieve your goals. Get off your couch and take a chance at this today.

Generate passive income

The joy one gets from living solely off one's rental income is immense and you deserve to be one of the few people who reach this reality. You need to dig your heels in, put the vision before you, and keep running towards it.

"Do not wait: the time will never be 'just right.' Start where you stand, and work with whatever tools you may have at your command and better tools will be found as you go along."

— Napoleon Hill

www.ingramcontent.com/pod-product-compliance
Lightning Source LLC
Chambersburg PA
CBHW030540220526
45463CB00007B/2923